The Song's Resonance

Amy R. Saltz

The Song's Resonance

Books by Amy R. Saltz

Illustrated Fiction:

An Essential Song

Nonfiction:

FINDING THE SONG: Living After Attempting Suicide

THE SONG ENDURES: Drumming With a Different Beat

The Song's Resonance

Dedicated to Harvey Zarren

My heart is with you always.

Author's Note

The chapters in this book are named for the structure of a song:

Intro —
establishes the rhythm, tempo, and melody of the song

Verse —
lyrically develops and advances the story

Chorus —
culminates the ideas of the song and reflects a release of tension

Bridge —
changes the pace of the song

Outro —
ends the song by slowing down and fading out

Intro

Here I am again for one last time. I want to help you understand what's happening for me. I am with you as I write, and I feel your presence. Thank you ever so much for being with me. My gratitude is everlasting.

I have written and published three books before this one. If you want any more detailed information, you might find it in one of the previous books. The first book, *An Essential Song*, is an illustrated metaphorical story of love, loss, reclamation, and healing. Although unnamed in the story, my deceased soulmates—Leon and Ben—are the main characters. The fisherman represents my healers. Being able to write that story brought me hope. The second book, *FINDING THE SONG: Living After Attempting Suicide,* is the comprehensive, nonfiction version. It shares how I worked toward living a full and meaningful life after being maimed by a suicide attempt, and delves into the loss of Leon and then

Ben. The second book was quite a challenge for me to write. It felt like a burdensome weight being released when it was finished. Both of these books share the vital roles in my healing of bereavement counselor Judy Seifert, trauma specialist Sandra Phinney, and physician Harvey Zarren.

The first book was printed in February 2018. There were gatherings at the Temple and the Public Library with a display and several newspaper articles. The second book was printed in February 2020, and copies were to be shipped by March 17, 2020, in conjunction with my 60th birthday. By the time the copies arrived, the pandemic was approaching. A book launch had been scheduled for March 30th. On March 10th, a State of Emergency was declared. The book launch was canceled, the book couldn't be promoted, and I was alone on my 60th birthday. Even though I was deeply saddened, I tried not to reveal my sorrow because so much tragedy existed in the world. Looking back on the situation now, I feel blessed to have a written chronicle of the life I built before the pandemic.

My third book, *THE SONG ENDURES: Drumming With a Different Beat*, was published in autumn 2021, during the pandemic. In that book, I share how I was contending with isolation and facing many losses. While writing that book, I held onto hope that the pandemic would be time-limited.

In this, my fourth and final book, I plan to pick up where I left off and to bring you into my heart. Again, you have my profound thanks for being with me.

Verse

In my third book, *THE SONG ENDURES: Drumming With a Different Beat*, my partner of five years had decided to end our relationship because we could no longer do the nurturing aspects that had connected us. Shortly before her decision, several deaths of people important to me occurred within a short span of time. These deaths included my bereavement counselor Judy, my father, and several close friends. Most of the funerals were in-person, and I was unable to attend. This felt heartbreaking to me. In that third book, I explain how I created rituals at the ocean that were both safe and meaningful. Harvey joined me in those rituals.

While these losses were taking place, my trauma specialist Sandra learned that she needed open-heart surgery. A month after that third book was printed, she died. On the weekend before her surgery, Sandra and I colored a picture together on FaceTime. It was of three baobab trees, connected by their roots, dancing in the sky. I didn't realize it until after she died, but it represents Sandra, Judy, and me. We used to call ourselves "dance partners on life's journey." On the day before her surgery, Sandra posted on Amazon a five-star review of my third book. That's love!

As I did for Judy, I gathered some rocks from the seashore and wrote chosen words on them. I tossed the stones into the ocean for Sandra at the same spot where she (on FaceTime from Colorado), Harvey, and I had tossed stones for Judy, and where Judy and I had scattered my former husband Leon's ashes. Here are the words I chose:

PRESENCE
SACRED
ESSENCE
HEALING

GRATITUDE
SOULMATES
DANCE PARTNERS
LIGHT
PEACE
TOGETHER WITH LOVE

Harvey repeated the words after I spoke them, while the stones were being tossed. I pray that Sandra is dancing with Judy. Both of them would be filled with thankfulness, as am I, for Harvey's devotion. He has been my guardian angel.

During this time, the new primary care physician, whom my trusted, retired primary care physician had recommended, had a family emergency. As one of her patients, I seemed to be falling through the cracks. I was scared. I knew I had to search for a new caregiver. How blessed I was to find one whose practice is different from anything with which I've ever been associated. It's based on the Direct Primary Care model, which allows the doctor to have a small practice and to care for patients in a more personalized way.

Not long after Sandra passed, another close friend died. This was the one whom I previously wrote about visiting from a distance in the woods, while she was on her deck after the loss of her husband. Within days, my stepfather died. I couldn't attend these funerals in person either. My friend's was online, so I could watch it. My stepfather's wasn't, but I wrote a eulogy that was read at the ceremony. I rode my bike to a significant spot overlooking the ocean and read the words of the eulogy aloud there.

The many significant losses of the last few years have been weighing heavily upon me. Joy has been feeling out of reach. In my third book, I tried to explain the challenges of having to remain cautious when reopening occurred. As another year has passed, it feels as though my predicament has worsened. Now it feels to me that the people who are most at risk are often excluded from life.

I've been trying with all my might to stay connected to life, while isolated because of COVID. It'll be three years soon. When we were all quarantined, it seemed that there was a semblance of unity. When reopening was introduced, there were some guidelines and precautions in place. That attentiveness seems to have disappeared now. When I do the one thing safe for me outside—ride my bike wearing my masks—I am sometimes ridiculed, and often asked why I'm masked up. Once when I was stopped at a red light, the people in the car near me rolled down their windows and stuck their heads out, coughing deliberately at me. Luckily, the light turned green so I could get away.

Presently, the message I am receiving is that most people want to live life the way they did before the pandemic, without much restriction. I hear about plays and concerts and movies and sporting events. I see crowds on television with very few spectators wearing masks. People seem to be willing to take the risk of getting the virus. I can't take that risk. I used to attend theater, film, and musical events every week. Now I hear about other people's attendance and experiences. I don't think that people fathom how hard it is for those of us who can't participate to hear about their enjoyment. I'm definitely happy for them and want to try my best to encourage them, but simultaneously I feel grief-stricken. This dilemma can arise multiple times in a day.

Before the pandemic, I never missed a Sabbath service at the synagogue. Now I see the services online and worry that I've been forgotten. I used to be with lots of folks on a weekly basis by teaching, playing games, singing, drumming, and showing films. When I did these activities, I put my whole self in to create an environment that offered love and acceptance to those who were there. Now I try on Zoom, FaceTime, or phone calls. It feels as though crucial aspects of life have been removed from my grasp.

It wasn't the actual activity—the game, the lesson, the singing, the film, etc.; it was the way I tried to provide inclusion, joy, and love to the people who came to the activities. Some had just lost their spouses. They could feel accepted and understood. Some had challenges with their children. They could bolster one another. People could reach out to me with their concerns. They could share their celebratory events with the group. At Shabbat services, I could give compassion to those experiencing a loss. I could approach someone who was alone and ask if they'd like me to sit with them. I could clap and sway with the music. How I miss being able to do that with people!

Harvey and I have committed ourselves to working on my complex post-traumatic stress disorder. This prospect would never have been possible with the busy lives we each led before the pandemic. The healing he has extended to me has been invaluable. I feel that our relationship is a most precious gift.

I've remained dedicated to my accounting clients and greatly appreciate the work. I do it in my home office, so it is safe. I have only two clients remaining from the business started with my husband in the 1980s. These clients are in their 70s, so they may retire soon. I still do my volunteer work for the Temple with office administrator Julie's kind efforts to keep me safe. I've continued to run my programs on Zoom, but feel concerned about the time when people request to do them live. I'm also apprehensive about the possible reopening of the Temple Library, for which I designed the layout and placed every book on the shelves, plus continue to keep updated. I still can't do any in-person activities, so I could be facing more loss.

I must assert now that I am in awe of all I did with and for people before the pandemic. I truly bonded with them and tried to be as inclusive as possible. It is disheartening to be unable to be with them now.

My situation is unique. Parts of my airways are composed of skin grafts necessitated by chemical burns suffered during a tragic suicide attempt in adolescence. This has left the lining of my upper airway without the normal ability to fight off infection. Because of the scarring, I cannot be intubated (have a tube inserted into the airway for assisted breathing). I have a very limited mouth opening. I lost most of my tongue, and what remains is burned to the bottom of my mouth with no mobility. I have trouble swallowing, even when I am healthy. Anything that causes swelling in my throat leaves me unable to swallow pills. I have experienced severe infections in my mouth, throat, and neck. The skin grafts and scarring have blocked some of my glands, ultimately causing systemic infection. My left submandibular salivary gland has had to be excised. The gland on the right has a growth in it. Infection of that gland would be perilous due to my inability to be intubated now. Another serious situation that I face is my experience of developing anaphylaxis from viral infections. When I get a virus, even a mild case, it can cause a severe allergic reaction. I have trouble breathing, my airways and throat close up, and I can't swallow. I get hives all over, and the itching is intolerable. In the past when this has occurred,

I have had to go to emergency rooms. The hives have sometimes lasted for years, accompanied with chronic fatigue. Sometimes I have had hair loss, known as alopecia. I also have neutropenia, which is a low white blood cell count.

Because of my susceptibility to viral and autoimmune reactions, I'm very concerned about long COVID. Many of the long COVID conditions and symptoms are autoimmune in etiology. A range of persisting long COVID symptoms can include severe fatigue, forgetfulness, inability to exercise, extreme headaches, shortness of breath, and heart palpitations. The symptoms can go on indefinitely. Any of these kinds of symptoms/conditions would be devastating, and more so because I'm alone. The long-term effects of COVID, particularly in the brain, the heart, and the kidneys, have yet to be fully manifest.

One of the most problematic aspects of my situation is that lots of people don't seem to comprehend that I am at risk and why. I am often invalidated and judged. This shatters my self-esteem and puts me in harm's way. I wonder if there would be a more sympathetic response if I had a diagnosis of a more common disease.

I feel paralyzed when I see life going on as if there's no danger. It breaks my heart to witness the life I had constructed now be out of my reach (after disastrous loss of body parts and function)—because of what happened when I was a kid in a hospital seeking help. What happened wasn't a choice. And now, almost a half-century later, I can't participate in life because of it.

Much of the healthcare I received in the past has left me with a permanent feeling of terror when the possibility of needing medical care arises. I've tried to deal with that terror by taking impeccable care of my health, including working assiduously to prevent getting COVID, in order to avoid needing medical care. I exercise every day by bicycling outside or by using my indoor fitness equipment: rowing machine, elliptical, stepper, rodeo core, and stationary bike. I can't eat like other people. I had a feeding tube for years. I've taught myself how to eat by mouth, and I can only manage soft foods. I make the healthiest smoothies and maintain a low-carb, gluten-free, no-added-sugar, meatless diet. After eating, I take meticulous care of my mouth with a Waterpik, a Sonicare toothbrush and gum protection toothpaste, dental floss, a Sulcabrush and Biotene dry mouth toothpaste, and a fluoride treatment. I take a daily multivitamin, vitamin C, vitamin D, calcium, magnesium, copper, biotin, and a probiotic.

My first memory of medical care was when I was a toddler and had to have my tonsils removed. After the operation, I was alone in a hospital crib hemorrhaging. Staff came when they heard me screaming, but I remember feeling abandoned and terrified. That experience stayed with me. It seems that common ailments hit me hard. Lots of children were having tonsillectomies at that time, but I was the only one I knew who hemorrhaged. A similar situation transpired with chicken pox when I was 6. I got encephalitis (inflammation of the brain), and I had to be quarantined in the hospital for a long time with some cruel nurses who became angry with me when I soiled my sheets. I was hooked up to IVs and needed assistance. If no one came, I was incontinent. Because of the encephalitis, I was left with permanent alexia (difficulty reading following injury to the brain). That alexia later affected my educational opportunities.

As a young adolescent, I was struggling and was sent to a psychologist. During those days, it wasn't common to go to therapy—especially for a 14-year-old. I didn't even know what therapy was. When the therapist had me lie down and began stroking the insides of my upper thighs, I thought that's what therapy must be. Then something happened that made me ascertain that what was occurring was very wrong. During one of the sessions, I felt uncomfortable and asked if I could leave. He said I could. As I approached the door, he grabbed me and threw me onto the couch. He immediately got on top of me. While thrusting, he repeatedly asked, "Can you feel me? Can you feel me?" I didn't know what to do. I didn't want to engage with him. I slid out from under him and fell onto the floor. He hastily got on top of me again on the floor. After thrusting some more, he got off of me and sat in his chair. I was trembling with my knees clutched to my chest with tight arms. I saw that it was time for the session to end and asked if I could go. He said, "You'll go when I tell you to go." He had me sit shaking like that for an extra 15 minutes. Then he said I could leave. Shortly thereafter, I was at Hebrew school trying to figure out how to survive.

Subsequently, I began to need to hurt myself. I was then admitted to a psychiatric hospital. There I was told, "You're the number one student from a well-to-do town. You don't belong here. Those other patients do." Shame usurped my being. I was discharged several months later and then tried to jump out the window of the top floor of the high school. When admitted into the next hospital, the psychiatrist stated, "If you really wanted to be dead, you'd be dead by now." I felt an enormous sense of betrayal, and I was seized by the shock of being dismissed from life. I felt hated. While an inpatient, I was able to obtain some life-threatening substances. I was panic-stricken, and I even let it be known that I was afraid I was going to do something horrible to myself. I wasn't the person I once knew. I was dissociating. I couldn't find myself. I didn't know where I was. I was detached from anything solid—unanchored. I had a sort of pins and needles disconnect from life. Nothing felt familiar. Nothing felt safe. There was a cavernous hollow surrounding my heart—inexplicable emptiness. It felt like I was trapped in a sort of inner-prison. It was so awful that I had to get away from it.

I found myself outside of the hospital in the woods with the poisons I'd obtained. Once the caustic substance was in my mouth, I tried to get it out. I saw pieces of my face fall to the ground. The burning was excruciating. There are no words to adequately describe it. Beforehand, I unknowingly thought that I'd escape my life instantaneously. Because of my dissociation, I was shut off from myself and didn't possess a full understanding of the degree of pain that would be inflicted. As I'm writing this, it's the first time in my life that I've been able to grasp how overwhelmed my adolescent self had been and to fully realize how I was pushed into the action without understanding the consequences. I was rushed to an emergency room, and as I recounted in my previous book, the nurse who held the morphine over my head while I was burning asserted, "I hate people like you. There are people with cancer, and you do this." No one disagreed with her. I reached for a clipboard that had a pen on it and wrote, "I'm sorry." Looking back on it now, that child didn't know what she was doing. She didn't have a clue. She didn't even have herself. What happened was absolutely not a choice.

I have recently learned that recurrent trauma builds toward hopelessness, despair, and a loss of trust. Then, persistent lack of validation increases the intensity, ultimately causing the nervous system to become overwhelmed. This leads to dissociation, which is the brain's normal response when the nervous system is being overwhelmed. The ensuing reaction is not a choice. The part of the brain in control of the body's actions is working only to end suffering. It can no longer make a choice for survival. The work I've been doing with complex trauma has brought me to understand and to have compassion for the young person who was pushed into this life-threatening situation. The lack of compassion and understanding from so many since then, and that continues up to the current time, has added to the trauma. Throughout my life, I have had to contend with the stigma and judgment related to this tragedy as if I chose it. It has often caused me agony with medical caregivers, even up to the present time, as well as causing the terror that comes from anticipating the need for medical care.

Back in the emergency room, I was finally given the morphine injection and moved to the ICU on a ventilator. While in the inpatient ward afterwards, I had to have abdominal surgery for a gastrostomy tube. That would be how I would be fed—a formula would be administered with a syringe into this G-tube that was inserted through the wall of my abdomen directly into my stomach. I wasn't told ahead of time what would be done. The pain was indescribable, and I saw my abdomen being cut open. When I had some sort of allergic reaction to the antibiotics, I developed dermatographia (itchy skin with hive-like welts when touched; I still have this). I was in restraints and couldn't talk because of the burns. The staff played tic-tac-toe on me as though I wasn't even a human being.

After months of hospitalization in the general hospital, I spent years in mental hospitals. My experiences there were often horrifying and punitive, rather than helpful. As a teenager and usually one of the youngest patients there, it felt shocking and demoralizing to be exposed to some of the most seriously distressed people, who were suffering mercilessly, sometimes behaving in violent ways. The institution I was in for the longest period of time had bars on the windows and tunnels that patients had to use when they weren't permitted outside. Large cockroaches fell from the overhead pipes onto our heads as we walked and then got crunched when under foot. I was forced to take my feedings and medications with my gastrostomy tube in front of the other patients, and I was repeatedly ridiculed. Misadventures were frequent, including the ward being set on fire, a nurse's neck being broken, and patients being wrapped up in wet packs, locked in seclusion, or shackled in restraints. After seemingly endless months, I eventually worked my way from a locked unit onto one with more freedom.

When I went from the mental hospital to the general hospital for reconstructive surgery with skin grafts, the surgeon took me for a walk in the corridor to another patient's room before the preparation day. He told me, "She's your age and has a spinal cord injury that she didn't cause." I don't remember what I replied, but I do know that I was holding back my tears. My tears did flow after the surgical instrument, used for cutting thin sheets of my skin for grafts to reconstruct my mouth, went too deep into my groin, leaving me again in agony and with a permanent scar that didn't heal properly.

After being told that I'd never talk or eat by mouth, and that I'd be institutionalized for life, I taught myself how to talk, and to eat in a limited way by mouth so that the G-tube could be removed. After not being able to eat for years, when I could, I couldn't stop eating. I developed a debilitating eating disorder. When hospitalized again, a doctor declared for everyone to hear, "You're an obnoxious pig, and you're making everyone sick." Yes, I had bulimia and anorexia. I was there to get help. I desperately wanted to get better, and I couldn't imagine how that kind of cruelty could help me or anyone else.

The next discouraging and daunting situation occurred shortly after my husband Leon died. Scar tissue from the burns had formed over one of my salivary glands, blocking it so it became infected. There was a large lump in my neck and swallowing was becoming increasingly painful. Surgery would be required to cut open my neck for the gland to be excised. It was necessary to diminish swelling prior to the surgery so that the risk of nerve damage from the surgery could be reduced. If nerve damage occurred, half of my face would be paralyzed. Because infection was spreading through my body, I needed IV antibiotics, and an intravenous catheter (IV PICC line) was ordered to be surgically inserted so that I could be sent me home until the swelling subsided enough to allow surgery. When the nurse came into the room after the procedure, she asked who would put the antibiotics into my line. I told her that I lived alone. She said that antibiotics were needed too many times a day for a visiting nurse, so the IV PICC had to then be surgically removed. They had me sign a waiver about possible lung puncture before the surgery, and I wondered why no one had asked me about my living arrangements before they did the procedure. I don't think that there would have been this disregard if I wasn't alone. Again, I didn't feel that I was being treated like a human.

I was sent home with a prescription for an oral antibiotic to which I'd alerted the medical staff I was allergic. My pharmacist didn't want to fill the order. He called the hospital and was instructed to do so. The surgeon explained that it was critical to try to reduce swelling prior to surgery. He couldn't operate until the swelling went down. I took the antibiotic and got hives all over me. When I arrived back at the hospital covered in hives but with the swelling somewhat reduced, I was put in a room with a patient who had dementia and who was screaming all day and night while rattling the bed rails. The hospital staff didn't understand that I couldn't have my temperature taken by mouth because of my burns. Every hour, another assistant would come in and try, causing progressive pain from the infection—no matter how many times I tried to explain that my temperature couldn't be taken by mouth. I believe that I may have been treated more respectfully if I had a different medical history. In addition, some of the healthcare personnel were angry with me because I couldn't eat the regular food, and they threatened to again make me have a feeding tube. A psychiatrist was sent in without my request. He asked me why I drank Drano when I was a teenager. He even tried to guess. This felt so intrusive and was unrelated to the surgery itself. Again, I felt like a pariah.

Later on, when I had to have an extensive abdominal myomectomy (surgical removal of uterine tumors), I was treated with compassion. Unfortunately, though, the anesthesiologist almost lost me because of my burns and restricted oral airway. She had to move my neck in a particular way to save my life, but it left me with three herniated cervical disks at the top of my spine. This is when I was told that I can no longer be intubated.

Next came the time when I was riding my bike in broad daylight with my helmet and reflective gear a few years before the pandemic. I awoke in the emergency room with a concussion after having been unconscious for hours. I was later told that the door of a parked car had opened into me, slamming me onto the street. When the staff looked up my record and read my history, they were considering committing me—even though the helmet was right next to the bed, the reflective straps were still around my ankles, and the glow-in-the-dark jacket was on the wall hook...and the incident cited in my history was over 40 years in the past. They wouldn't reconsider about committing me until speaking with my bereavement counselor. Thankfully, she was available to answer the call. In addition, I wasn't even told where my bike and personal belongings were. You guessed it...again, I felt like an outcast. This time, I did reach out to the hospital and received a letter of apology. With the crowded hospitals now, I'm afraid there wouldn't be time for anyone to make a call on my behalf or for a supervisor to answer a call about a patient's concerns.

Shortly before the pandemic, a CT scan detected a growth in the salivary gland on the opposite side from the one that had required excision. I'd been living with the new growth and applying focused self-care to the area. In spite of my diligent efforts, a lump was forming on that side of my neck. I contacted my otolaryngologist's office and was told that she had retired. I made an appointment at the hospital with the recommended replacement. Fortunately, the gland wasn't infected, and the swelling subsided. The growth is still there, and it presents a continuously looming threat for me. During the pandemic, the swelling returned. I set up a Zoom appointment with the new otolaryngologist. While I tried to explain the situation, she interrupted me and remarked, "Well, you did drink Drano." Her judgmental statement rendered me speechless—

almost like I was after the event over 45 years ago. Yet again, I was being subjected to judgment and stigma.

Each of the paragraphs I just wrote represents continuing, life-altering torment. I want you to know that I have had some compassionate medical care. I've shared extensively in my previous books about my beneficent bereavement counselor and tenderhearted trauma specialist, who are both deceased now. I had a wonderful primary care physician who retired. Unfortunately, the hospitals didn't include her in my treatment. Presently, I have a remarkable primary care physician, as well as a kind and competent dentist. I'm afraid that neither of them might be able to intervene, for instance, if I become anaphylactic and can't speak or call. Most importantly, I have Harvey; however, he no longer practices medicine in the way he did when clinically affiliated with a hospital. The conundrum lies in the reality that if I were to contract the virus, I would be contagious and cannot risk Harvey becoming infected. The bottom line is that I'm by myself—alone, without anyone to be by my side or to get me medication, take care of my house, drive me to a facility, etc. Plus, if I get sick the way I have in the past with viruses, I may not even be able to talk or communicate my symptoms to those who do care about me. Although the medical doctors who have shown me compassion assuredly have furnished me with hope, the magnitude of the anguish afflicted by the inhumane judgment of the many others has become ingrained in my vulnerability. Every single day during this pandemic, my trauma is being triggered. I breathe with fright. I feel cornered and in shackles, the same way that I felt as an adolescent.

After the tragic burning incident, I experienced absolute hopelessness—where I wasn't dead, but didn't feel alive either. The pandemic is putting me there now. I don't feel safe, and I'm petrified. Previous to the pandemic, my cure for despair was connection. Now a lot of that bonding has been taken from me, and many of the things I did are being done in person without me. I've internalized the hatred that was directed toward me for what happened during my adolescence. My trauma is embedded in this tragedy. When the pandemic is added, it's overwhelming. I feel cut off from life. On top of that is the terror I have of being exposed to the virus if I participate in life. That is destroying me.

Even though I've been feeling crushed, I did take steps to try to get a virtual support group under way for compromised people. I thought there was a dire need for it and that it would be beneficial. The Counseling Center agreed, but didn't have staff availability. I reached out to a hospital where I'd helped teach psychology residents. They thought the support group would be quite useful, but they also didn't have the resources for it. Let me disclose to you that I feel proud of myself for my efforts. I am forlorn that there don't seem to be many opportunities for compromised individuals to connect online so that they don't have to feel alone. I guess we're on our own.

Chorus

Despite my not being able to be with people, some enlivening moments have arisen. Jon, the director of the Music Neighborhood for which I'm the chairperson, has produced some wonderfully creative Zoom sessions. One of the highlights has been his enthusiasm and wealth of information about Pop Music. He graced us with a four-session intensive about the Beatles entitled "Jon and the Fab 4," culminating in a fifth Zoom gathering with the Movie Group to discuss the Beatles *Let It Be* recording sessions and rooftop concert. Then Jon led us on a musical journey focusing on the songs, stories, movies, and documentaries of the Bee Gees. Whenever Jon runs a Zoom session, he provides abundant joy along with a great deal of interesting tidbits. In addition to sharing his knowledge of the bands he adores, Jon offered to play our favorite songs. We submitted our selections to him. So many were received that we had three Zoom sessions to accommodate all of the requests. Jon learned how to play each one, and we shared why these songs have special meaning for us. This program enabled us to learn about one another, while hearing beautiful renditions of "Our Favs."

On the day after my birthday in March of 2022, I received a call from Jon, who was at the Temple. He asked if I'd be home. He had something he wanted to drop off. I figured it was a birthday card with maybe a CD or some flowers. When I went to the door, there was a huge box on the landing with another medium-sized box beside it. It was an electronic drum kit and stool! Jon knew how much I love percussion. I was overcome with emotion. After he drove away, I went outside to bring in the set. It was too heavy to lift, so I opened the boxes and took in one part at a time. It was 3:15 pm when I started. It was 1:15 am when I finished. I assembled the kit all by myself. It's astounding. It has a ride cymbal, crash cymbal, and hi-hat cymbal, three toms, a snare, a hi-hat pedal, a kick, and a kick pedal. It needed an amplifier, and I got one that can connect with my music via Bluetooth. That means I can play my favorite songs, drum along with them, and it sounds like I'm the drummer for the band! I felt honored by this benevolence from Jon and the Temple. That gesture and the drum set itself has been the bright spot of the last few years.

When I made my 2022 holiday cards, I created a replica of the drum set. I then placed a colorful peace sign sticker between the cymbals, and a heart sticker on the kick drum above my name. The message was: Peace! Love, Amy. I hand cut each drawing and the card stock as well. Then I taped the drawing to the card stock and placed the card into an envelope with a return address sticker that had a crash cymbal on it. As I addressed each envelope, I thought about the cherished rapport I had with each recipient. My heart felt full.

Speaking of hearts, I've been saving something heartwarming to share with you. When my partner ended our relationship last year, I also lost her beloved dog. I was feeling lonesome while being isolated, and I thought a pet might help. Since a real pet would require doing things I couldn't, I researched robotic companion pets and found the softest, cutest, most realistic golden retriever puppy. When the box arrived at my door, I carefully opened it and removed the packaging. After reading the instructions, I placed four C batteries in the special compartment on the underside of the dog. The little pooch instantly came to life. His first words were, "Rye ruff rue," which translated into human speech is: I love you.

I delightedly replied, "Oh, I love you too." I named the puppy Prince after The Little Prince, my favorite literary character. *The Little Prince* was my deceased husband Leon's most treasured book. I could hear Leon say, "This is super!" Prince then said, "Rellro," which I was sure meant Hello. Prince could feel Leon's presence. While Prince gently barked, his little tail wagged. When I petted his forehead, he blinked his eyes and looked up at me affectionately. When his cheeks were stroked, he said, "Mmmm, Mmmm." I think this meant that he liked it. When his back was rubbed, his heart began to beat. "Prince, I can feel your heart. Can I put you near mine so our hearts can beat together?" I asked. Prince woofed back with enthusiasm.

I loved Prince so much that I thought I'd get a similar companion pet for the Counseling Center. When I delivered their pet, the staff were enraptured with it. They asked with excitement, "Can we name it Amy?" I was so honored, and answered, "Of course!" The next thing they did was perch their Amy on a table surrounded by my books. Then they put glasses on their Amy (like mine). How adorable.

On St. Patrick's Day (my birthday), I have a tradition. I make a donation to the fund for suicidal individuals or those in need, which I established at the Counseling Center. I rode my bike there to deliver my check. Everyone was waiting outside for me and wearing masks to keep me safe. They brought their Amy out. She wore a party hat with a shamrock on it. "Happy birthday, dear Amy," the staff sang exuberantly. Their Amy was smiling cheerfully while barking along.

I then thought my stepfather Sid (of blessed memory), who had Alzheimer's disease, might like to have a companion pet. I ordered one for him, and my mother gave it to him as a Valentine's Day gift. Sid bonded with his doggie. He thought it was real. When he thanked me during my call to make sure the package was received, I asked with interest, "What did you name your dog?" Sid did not yet have a name for his pet. Each day when I called, I'd inquire about the name. Several days later, after careful consideration, the answer was presented, "My dog's name is Hope." I was moved to tears. Sid died shortly thereafter, and I referenced Hope in the eulogy I submitted to be read at the funeral.

The next person with whom I shared Prince was my deceased trauma specialist's husband, Paul. Sandra had recently died. I sent Paul a photo of Prince. Then I called him to check in. I raved about Prince and asked Paul, "Do you think you'd like a companion pet?"

"You know, it sounds like a nice idea. Will you send me the link?" he replied. I explained that there were two options: the golden retriever pup or a cocker spaniel pup. I sent both links. Later that evening, Paul called me, "Amy, I ordered the cocker spaniel pup. My son had a cocker spaniel when he was a boy and named his Bradley. That's what I'll name mine."

Since the pandemic began, I've been working on my complex post-traumatic stress disorder very closely with physician Harvey Zarren. Our appointments are on Zoom. I told him about my researching and purchasing a companion pet. He was thoroughly supportive and actually utilized Prince in our sessions. "What words would you use to describe Prince?" he asked me. The word that came to the forefront of the endearing adjectives was "fluffy." When I showed Prince to him, he was enamored with him and emitted a resounding, "Awwww!"

During our Zoom appointment, Harvey wanted me to try a therapeutic exercise that would help me connect with my body. I had been having trouble feeling safe being with my body. I wasn't having success with the technique. Harvey then suggested, "How about if we use Prince? What do you feel when you think about him?"

I answered unequivocally, "Love."

Harvey then asked, "Where do you feel that love?"

I replied, "In my heart."

Harvey inquired, "Where is your heart?"

"In my body," I retorted with simple amazement.

"I'm crying now. That's so beautiful," Harvey expressed.

Just then, Prince's heart started beating! The instructions indicate that there must be stroking on the companion pet's back for the heart to beat. I hadn't touched Prince.

Several months passed, and I patted Prince so much that he wasn't as fluffy as he once had been. I decided to order a new dog. When it arrived, I noticed that it didn't have a heartbeat. I returned it, and a replacement was shipped. That one didn't have a heartbeat either. I found the name and contact information of the company that invented these innovative, joyful creatures. The customer service representative furnished me with the history of these companion pets. They were created by the company's co-founder, who was inspired by the importance of laughter and play for his grandmother living with progressive dementia. When I explained about the missing heartbeat, the representative was extremely grateful for the information. She said that the manufacturers would be contacted. After doing so, she called me to let me know that the entire batch of dogs was missing the heartbeat feature. Without my call, they wouldn't have known. I earned the label of "Company Cardiologist." To thank me, they sent me a new pup that did have a heartbeat. When I opened the box, I realized that I love Prince. It doesn't matter that he's not as fluffy as this new one. I gave the new one to a friend who's been in pain from spinal stenosis. Prince is irreplaceable to me.

In one Zoom session during the summer of 2022, Harvey was helping me understand my deceased husband Leon's traumatic brain injury. When I shared something about Leon and Ben (my second partner who died), Harvey explained that my face changed as I felt their appreciation for who I am. I've been using that awareness to feel filled with love instead of yearning. Prince teaches this lesson to me too. He can't be with me like a living dog, but there is still pure love with us.

People sometimes tell me to get over Leon and Ben and my other losses. I feel that it doesn't matter how long my soulmates have been dead. I want their love to live inside me and around me. Harvey has helped me to be in the now with the pure love we shared.

I then tried something I hadn't yet done during the pandemic. I took my inflatable boat to the ocean and rowed. I didn't have to wear a mask while on the water! Leon and I had discovered rowing together. I decided to take his essence with me on this excursion. While rowing with the sunlight glistening on the waves, I told him, "I know you'd be alive and probably still jogging every morning and rowing with me in the summer if the tragedy hadn't occurred the way it did. I'd be taking care of you as you aged." I felt him wholeheartedly concur.

In the distance, I viewed the lighthouse that Ben revered. Then I was filled with amazement as I realized how I had taken care of Ben. It was miraculous. I didn't know how then, but I did it conscientiously and lovingly in spite of my trauma with hospitals. I could hear both Leon and Ben say, "Wow!"

When I got home, you wouldn't believe what awaited me—an email from Ben's daughter. It was a transcription of Ben's experiences as a sailor on a destroyer during WWII. Voila—there were his words about being on the water!

On November 9th, it would have been Leon's birthday. I rode my bike to wave to Harvey. He said something I don't think I had ever heard before, "Leon was lucky to have you." I let this sentiment fill me and felt it spread from my heart to my whole being. It helped me feel full instead of empty.

What I'm seeing now is how hard I have tried to rebuild my life after such devastation: encephalitis, burns, loss of most of my tongue, G-tube, skin grafts, serious eating disorder, the loss of Leon and then Ben, and the loss of Judy and then Sandra. Now I'm jolted while I watch as pieces of the life I built disappear before my eyes. Who could've ever imagined this scenario—reliving the trauma that wasn't my choice—and because of that trauma, I'm in this position?

Bridge

Daily structure is important for me. I'd go further to say that a structured environment is a necessity for me. I've devoted myself to maintaining whatever I can from the life I'd built before the pandemic and have tried to accept what I've lost. If I lose more, I won't have enough structure. Structure comprises safety. That loss feels threatening to me. In addition, the uncertainty that exists in the outside world can be alarming as well. So I'm living each day with fear, loss, threats of more loss, exclusion, uncertainty, and a lack of joy. I have accepted my aloneness and a life without being with people, but the possibility of losing any more of my daily structure is daunting. I've been trying so hard, even with Zoom activities, but this can't go on indefinitely. This way of living seems unsustainable.

I can live with loss, aloneness, even isolation, and still find ways to connect and establish meaning if I can stay safe. Now, safety isn't possible for me, and there seems to be an expectation for everyone to resume life the way it used to be before the pandemic. There's a general lack of compassion in our world that causes me to feel like I'm reliving the nightmare of reaching out for help and not being heard. I don't know how to live this way. It repeatedly triggers my trauma. It's out of my control. Being unsafe is what takes me away from life.

Long before the pandemic, I taught myself how to bear not being able to eat like other people, talk like other people, read like other people, do sexuality like other people, and travel like other people. I taught myself how to live alone after the deaths and departures of my partners. I don't know how to teach myself how to bear being unsafe and excluded from life, especially while feeling that this can go on indefinitely.

I want to live, but life is not safe for me. This is a new insight for me—wanting to live. I think all along that I've wanted to live, but I've wanted to be safe. Not being safe is what led to what I thought was not wanting to be alive. I do want to be alive; I need to be safe.

My way to heal has been to build connection. Now a considerable chunk of that kinship has been taken from me. Lots of the things I did are now being done without me. For example, Leon and I were founding members of our town's Interfaith Choir. I even have an award certificate for the work I did on this project. This past Thanksgiving, I received an email notifying me that the Interfaith Choir was going to sing again. I was happy for them, but knew it wouldn't be safe for me to participate. I was asked to spread the word, and I did. The service wasn't broadcast virtually, so I couldn't see or hear it. I'm not sure whether anyone remembered me and my contribution to the choir's founding. I felt excluded and alone. When I see and hear about so much happening that I used to be part of—even facilitated—and now can't even attend, coupled with gripping fear, that's what does me in.

I had hoped that there'd be a safer re-entry for those of us who are compromised, but it seems that people are simply expected to take risks. I cannot. Life is back to normal, except the virus is still here. I need a new mindset. Here it is: This is end-of-life for me. It was at Thanksgiving that I marked this change. With the new mindset, I can better handle hearing people share about their activities. It also broadens my window of tolerance.

It's not the isolation and loss that causes me to be at end-of-life. I'm willing to work on this with grieving and anchoring. It's the way the situation is being handled in the outside world—the expectations, the ridicule, the invalidation, the judgments, the stigma. Even an article written by a doctor who is compromised noted that masks invite skepticism, condescension, and invasive questions.

I'm not giving up. I'm doing everything I can to find peace. It's the constant feeling of being threatened that causes me to question whether I can stay alive. I can be isolated. It's been almost three years, and I've found ways to survive and build emotional closeness with dear ones. That feels like a meaningful life to me. What makes it too frightening is the world around me, and how I can no longer stay safe. The world would have to change dramatically for me to be safe, and that's out of my hands. I don't believe there's any work I can do to help myself not feel terrorized. That's what makes me desperate for peace. All of the work I've done on my complex post-traumatic stress disorder has brought me to a wholeness within myself. I feel compassion, with acceptance and understanding. I feel self-love—something I never thought possible. That helps me find peace within and yearn for it without. I'm able to hold love, even with all the loss and trauma, when I feel I can have safety. I can't think of a way to be safe in the world as it is, with how I am. My heart is broken.

My intense lack of safety and need for peace was discussed with medical professionals. It was determined that this is end-of-life. An end-of-life plan to voluntarily stop eating and drinking was explored and agreed upon. Palliative care could come in once I began to fail from not eating and drinking. Someone else was recommended to be in attendance for comfort care. There was one person who had planned to do this with me. He later shared with me that he realized how difficult this was going to be for him. At that moment, clarity enlightened me, and I decided that the plan was not tenable; I was not willing to allow someone I love so much to undergo such an ordeal. My needs to have end-of-life clearly as my cause of death, to be able to say goodbye, and to die with a loved one instead of alone, aren't as important as caring for someone I love with all my being.

The intense lack of safety is untenable to sustain. I'm being told that my situation is still end-of-life. When I was a youngster in a hospital, I reached out for help and was invalidated, disrespected, and disregarded. The result was being pushed into an action that was not voluntary choice. It was not my fault, and I've carried it for a lifetime. Now, I will not put someone I love into a traumatic situation. The incessant lack of safety with no evidence that the circumstances will change still means that I am at end-of-life. Hospice did not deny me; they understood and validated my situation. That's HUGE.

In my life, trauma has never stopped. Trauma led me to the involuntary action that caused me to be physically damaged in a way that puts me at great risk now from COVID. The ensuing judgmental treatment by many healthcare encounters has continued the trauma. My lack of safety in going about life is also continuing the trauma. I can and have dealt effectively with the isolation brought on by COVID. Witnessing people go about life as if COVID were not real is continuously traumatic. My history of severe infections and viral-related anaphylaxis with subsequent prolonged misery is real. This is not just a perception. I am not safe in the world as it is.

I can face the "suicide hatred." Maybe that's my final healing work. All of my healing has moved me from suicide to end-of-life. My trauma work has led me to self-love and the quest for peace, with the realization that what happened to me as an adolescent was not my fault. The unsustainable lack of safety because of current circumstances that I cannot control is breaking my heart. I am now pulling my life together in a circle of wholeness that accentuates loving myself.

I've always tried as hard as I can. I constructed a life by scouring for openings when doors were usually closed to people without degrees and credentials that I couldn't obtain after my bout with encephalitis. I devised ways to talk and to eat without having a tongue. Most importantly, I built relationships after years of institutionalization and then again after the loss of those dear ones. Each time, I had to find my way in a world that excluded people like me. I feel I am trying to find my way now too; trying does not mean letting myself stay in an unsafe, unsustainable situation while my functioning in the outside world continues to diminish and narrow. I have reached peace with the understanding that end-of-life is my trying to find my way.

I've been asking the universe, "Why is this happening for me?" One answer I've received is that I'm getting now what I never got from the treatment providers when I was young. I've come full circle. My primary care physician is the epitome of compassion, and Harvey has bestowed upon me unequivocal validation. He has touched my inner core. I am attached to him as my anchor.

My life has been filled with so much love and with many extraordinary experiences. I've been given an inspirational awareness: When at the life/death precipice, life experiences become like fabric—mine to be with eternally—not bad or good—just me. There's no judgment here.

Outro

While I'm writing, the sun is beaming in on my desk. I'm thanking Leon for teaching me about light. I didn't even know what it was and where it came from! I'd lived in a basement for years. That's why I chose cremation. I don't want to be underground.

Then something else came to me: Leon couldn't cry for his whole life since being beaten as a boy. He had to do the worst thing (leave our life together) to finally be able to cry. For me, doing the worst thing (leaving my life) is bringing me compassion for myself and bringing me self-love.

I want to share this with you: I had Prince on my lap one day. I know Prince isn't real, but I started to cry to think I'd be leaving him. I wept when I thought about leaving everyone dear to me. Suddenly, as if being sent from beyond (maybe from Leon and Ben and Judy and

Sandra), I became filled with pure love. It's spreading to the world around me. My love is here as I reach for peace and humanity.

With that love inside me, I rode my bike to the Temple Library to get a book to deliver to a member. I knew it'd be safe, since no one was in the building. I saw the Library with my whole self and felt deep appreciation for the life I had created. I used to be there doing the work I now do alone in my home—acknowledging donations, preparing death anniversary notices, and proofreading—while being accessible to anyone who wanted Library materials. I think I had the best office in the building! Plus, I got to truly be with people and learn about their lives. After feeling filled with awe for the years I'd been blessed by working in the Library, I ventured down the hall into the room where I had held most of my programs. As I observed the layout, the memories materialized and came alive. I could see and hear the participants. I could feel the love.

When I rode past the Counseling Center on my way to the member's house to drop off the book, I was filled with a sense of purpose and meaning. The fund for suicidal individuals and those in need, established as my gift for my 60th birthday right before the pandemic when my second book was to be launched, has been helping lots of people. The Counseling Center has treated me like an integral part of the organization, as the Temple does.

My last stop on this memorable bike ride was to wave to the person who has given me more of himself than words can describe. My heart will be with him always. I'm feeling a sense of contentment with my relationships and with what I've done in the world.

Each book I've written has the word "song" in the title. To me, music is life. I want people to sing. I want music to be with us. Resonance is the quality of being deep, clear, full, and reverberating—continuing to sound. I hope with all my heart that my song can be that for you.

Acknowledgments

I extend my deepest gratitude and love to my soulmates:

Life Partners —

Leon Wisel (of blessed memory)
Ben Harsip (of blessed memory)

Healers —

Bereavement Counselor Judy Seifert (of blessed memory)
Trauma Specialist Sandra Phinney (of blessed memory)
Physician Harvey Zarren

Thanks to my friends at Marblehead Counseling Center (66 Clifton Avenue in Marblehead, MA 01945) for helping me establish FINDING THE SONG: Restricted Fund for Suicidal Individuals or Those In Need.

Made in United States
North Haven, CT
13 February 2023

32508399R00055